SEPTEMBER

SEPTEMBER

Poems

RACHEL JAMISON WEBSTER

TriQuarterly Books
Northwestern University Press
Evanston, Illinois

TriQuarterly Books
Northwestern University Press
www.nupress.northwestern.edu

Printed in the United States of America

10 9 8 7 6 5 4 3 2 1

Library of Congress Cataloging-in-Publication Data
Webster, Rachel J.
    September : poems / Rachel Jamison Webster.
      p. cm.
    Collected poems, some previously published.
    ISBN 978-0-8101-5231-1 (pbk. : alk. paper)
    I. Title.
PS3623.E3976S47 2013
811.6—dc23

2012051060

In memory of Richard Fammerée

and to our daughter,

Adèle

CONTENTS

THREE

ACKNOWLEDGMENTS

Thanks to the editors of the following publications, where some of these poems first appeared:

Brute Neighbors: Urban Nature Poetry, Prose, and Photography: "Container Garden"

The Greensboro Review: "Maybe Gravity"

Mothering: "Milk"

M Review: "Bleeding Heart," "Cream of the Pour Is the Cream of Skin Thickening," "September You Become Me," "Through Hooded Clouds Untranslatable, Once"

Not a Muse: A World Poetry Anthology: "Eurydice," "Fired in the Body"

The Paris Review: "Pomme"

Perihelion: "American Terminal," "Late September"

Platte Valley Review: "Birth Is When We Recall Ourselves"

Poetry: "La Porte," "Dolphins at Seven Weeks," "Kauai"

Prairie Schooner: "Cheyenne," "Yom Kippur"

Rattle: "How Did We Come to Be the Ones Whose Feet Are Being Washed?," "When We Saw It"

The Southern Review: "At the DQ," "Early Childhood"

Wicked Alice: "Often She'd Drop into Fathomless"

"Eurydice," "Lingua," and "The Sea Came Up and Drowned" appeared in *The Blue Grotto,* a chapbook published in 2009 by Dancing Girl Press.

I would also like to thank the Northwestern University English Department, the Poetry Foundation, the Academy of American Poets, the Poetry Center of Chicago, and the Warren Wilson MFA Program for Writers for much needed support and encouragement, and the outstanding people at Northwestern University Press, especially the visionary and steadfast Parneshia Jones.

I am grateful to my parents Cynthia and Jim Webster for everything, including a dreamer's childhood beside woods and water. Thank you to my brother

Douglas for his laughter and comradeship, and to my loving grandparents, uncles, and aunts, especially Laurel Webster who built the playhouse, Marla Major who sent the books, and "Aunt Havisham" Cynthia Erskine who writes to remind me. Thank you to my friends Rachael Bergan, Julianna Vermeys, Karen Behm, Eula Biss, Lucy Anderton, Daniel Johnson, Jesse Lichtenstein, Bhikshuni Weisbrot, Stanzi Vaubel, Josie Raney, Kristina Goel, and Colleen Abel, many of whom read these poems in earlier stages, and to my mentors Mary Kinzie, Reginald Gibbons, Ellen Bryant Voigt, Anne Calcagno, and Carl Dennis.

SEPTEMBER

SEPTEMBER YOU BECOME ME

You shawl me like smoke.

My hands shake, I go down out the door hoping
no one will talk to me, ask me something

like my name. I can feel your hunger,
your question a bell plundered of its tongue.

Of course you can have my coffee,
can walk with me down the street to buy the *Times*.

I imagine you in parts and snag
on trash because this other, this

blinding fire and swim bladder sloshing
with rain—well, I have trouble
walking and counting out change.

You are still so present, I know
we share a mad passion for this autumn,
this light unburdened life.

See how my hands float before me.

Since you went the light is so clear
it has become everything.

Faces peel from the bricks.

And outside the impoverished city hospital
someone has planted an Easter lily.

Its trumpet erupts from green tongues.

White throat that is your life.

ONE

LINGUA

It started like this.
In delight. How could I

not see the leaves
ringing yellow with light,
taste the berry opening
on my tongue and not want

to tell you. If we
had never separated.

If we had gone on walking
hip to hip, then

just the extension of the arm, wonder
in the eyes, soft

fruit warm in the hand, passed from
my hand to yours, just this

would have been enough.

But I walked further to gather.
You crouched waiting in hunt and what

I saw was petals
opening, a quickened winging!

How could I not pursue it?
How could I not come back

to tell you with my nimble fingers
then a flutter of music on my tongue?

My first word was *look*
I met this missing
you—meet this—thus

an undercurrent of the word
is love.

WHEN WE SAW IT

It was early in morning's memory,
with that fog around the edges
and us wrapped in blankets, rocking

just up and over the rung of consciousness
into the blurred limbs we were coming
to know as our own, into the car

clapping through a broth of wind and rain,
parents murmuring in the front seat
over wiper beats and soft talk radio—

sounds to become the beginning
and end of love—a slow unwrapping
of cinnamon gum and her, passing it to him

as he aims us straight and low.
The car slows. Then stops.
She opens the door

to asphalt, soaped sky.
Across the road, a workman
is climbing the hotel sign.

He scales the tight white rungs
until he's high as the building,
until he's no longer

what we understand as a man
but something small enough to hold and bend
like an action figure, or poem.

Is this the moment, years later, when I say
the bag slung over his heart
is filled with black letters?

Is this when I have him pause
at the top, hot luck rushing his limbs
one March dawn, and how long

can I stare like this—
at his body, interrupted with mist,
his tiny hand reaching into his tiny bag,

and us, clutching orange juice,
still swaddling our newness
in this world, before we see it—

no no no
of a moment
dropping through

the hollow pole
of a life and it goes on
happening and yet

it happened almost slowly—
a man, falling
like no more

than a bright spoked
star of snow.
With us there,

trying to wake.

LEAVES

This world in its spiked beauty splits me
          into rhythm and shard the shivering
leaves break me into aching into all

of us holding pain in our limbs'
          liquid resistances and incremental
disappearances into remodelings

and earbuds brain medications
          and vacations and here I am again
crying behind my sunglasses.

Roses will open into a wall of the frost.
          Stunned pinks wet and rot.
Shadows and glow ribbon out from the trees

where a man and his son pass,
          back and forth, playing catch.
How can we not ache with everything

around us breathing and time
          dropping through our bodies like dust
and these last leaves—squash and mouth-

colored, each becoming
          singular in its wind-timbred fall?

THE INVERSION

Really something, the parents called him,
with his ready jokes and pedal boat.

He'd take kids out in it to the center
of the lake, over the whispering grasses,
past the marsh where the herons and alligator lived.

I was nine and shy and wild, always paddling
further than allowed in my own blue canoe.
I never intended to become an adult, to live as they did
according to some inner metronome of chores.

They kept returning to the same names and places
so I'd grown in multiples no one knew.
They saw only my skin and thought I lived
on that surface humming with light.

The day was bright, the black lake spotted
with lily pads large and flat as platters.

When his boat skimmed over them
it made the sound of a hand rubbing
methodically on nylon, sound against sound
of pedals whining desperately as bedsprings.

Across the lake, a woman laughed—
a low bird called out—
he had stopped us in the middle now,
where to those on shore we were miniature:
a pinch, a glint, a little anecdote long finished.

I was still and silent as an animal.
I did not scream or say no. I had not known
I could be one of the weak, and I let it enter me
dead-dry and chaffing in the old inversion

that makes the weak see the strong
from that long weary distance, and they look so small
in the smallness of what they will do.

I was underwater, I was swaying
like swamp grass, staring up
at an old fat man thinking, someday

he will see himself here,
and then he'll be human.
There will be no relief.

YOM KIPPUR

Blood in a jar pulsing
into feather into water and this
is the New Year.

We've made our ablutions.
We've burned with fever
and chanted and wondered
ourselves back toward One.

And now the fruit splits the tree
and leaves tongue to gold
and I dream I'm a dust-mote.

Everything is perfect in its easy sweep.

I have no idea in the dream of being
dust but only know I'm
in some central endless harmony.

Then in another
part of the dream I'm in your new house,
large and anonymous and clean.
All the bowls wiped to a sheen on the shelves.

And you are opening to show me
drawers of forks and knives,
quality flatware stacked high,
each piece having clicked into place.

What can I say?

The whole time I am wondering
what the utensils, empty chairs and plush carpets
really mean, if they are all different
shapes for the same thing,

and what it is they and we
are trying to say.

BLEEDING HEART

In that house there was a portal
under the porch that opened
onto parched earth glinting
with glass and old nails.

I kept the red wheelbarrow there
and once bringing it out saw
what must have been
all summer developing:

a three-foot stalk, lace-leafed,
fonting tongues and pearls—
and all of it pale
as cartilage or bonewater.

Somehow it had grown
only on air and inner fire
into a colorless double of its other,
pink and dripping in the border bed.

Its feminine shape burned my mind.
All that white!
I wish I had stood there and seen.
But revulsion seized me and

I pulled it out.
It collapsed as a stopped faucet
and dropped a smarting spine in the red bin, then
I covered it.

AMERICAN TERMINAL

In the dream we sit in a terminal
of bruised reds and blues, waiting.
It is understood we are not human
and I for one don't want to be there,
don't like these others who call themselves
my kind. If it is a banquet I don't remember
any food. It is more like what they call a shower.
We pass cheap products, vacuum-packed
and smelling of plastic. Nothing is worth wanting.
I can't even see the lucky one. Passers
pronounce the products' praises, suggest the gifts
will get consecutively better if we just stay seated.
Beside me is an older woman who does not care.
After hours of passing, I notice and speak to her,
but do so clumsily through the prop of her jacket.
Lovely! We like the same colors! something like that.
She stares a long way back to who I am.
Cheap shoes and scarves sliding through my hands.
When her daughter arrives to sit at her feet,
I, in the old presumption of kindness,
begin to introduce them, then think,
who am I to name anyone to anyone,
being as we are faces of the same sleep.

X

I admit in panic
I reach back sometimes
for its slipping sides, but I
jumped that ship
called my generation.

We were just children,
playing the handed-down game
of Battleship, sitting cross-legged
on yarn carpet, waiting
for the parents to get home.

You remember that
tedious grid, the red pegs
that never fit.

Kitchens linoleumed in olive and brick,
Wonder and the American dream gone stale,
and the heartland not admitting it,
and the family asleep in front of the TV.

I hid Bibles and self-help books
under the sink, behind the TP.

I didn't want my mother to think
I wasn't happy,
but I needed those things
to keep from killing myself.

I learned to die and rise
in a thousand daily ways instead.
I must have seemed sad
in my desperation not to seem sad.

Then Love found me.
Without it, I would still be mired
in dried leaves, knowing myself
by my melancholy.

Without it, my life would not
belong to me.

For the world is aglow with what it is
and what it cannot be.

And if I say I love
the stones by the shore
it means I love their stony forms and colors

and also the blindness
their shapes make
when laid against each other.

You could not love me
to life. Without this

I'd be back wandering
the heaps of hay, trying
to find a door in a hill.

I was delivered to the hill
in a dream.

It was part of the earth's body,
a curve furred with grass.

Beside it was the war
memorial everyone was
huddled under, listening

to the men who yelled best
the collective anger,
which was fear.

I looked into the hill.
There were a few people I knew there.

One approached from a great distance,
over the land.

She was tall and pregnant
and her hair shone like the wheat.

She said to me, I say now to you,
it is just like stepping into a room.

HOW DID WE COME TO BE THE ONES
WHOSE FEET ARE BEING WASHED?

Cassandra's beside me at the nail salon,
getting the dark parts of her feet sanded off.

Liver troubles turned my soles white, she says,
then pitch-black, and I want to get 'em back
to normal before summer comes.

I ask her if they hurt and she says, *Not too bad,*
I stayed on 'em every day at work, but that was just God,
lifting the heavy bags.

Vietnamese women razor-scrape
our heels, rub soap over our insteps and toes,
as Iraqi girls, suspended on the TV,
enter, shyly, their first school.

Uniformed in wool, they stand at scrapwood desks,
while outside, knuckles of flame
tear into a Hummer, burn to sludge steel,
ankle, sand, stomach,

and the network's panning back and forth
between the girls dutiful at their work
and the truck exploding, and one of us says, how beautiful
the people there are. How now they will never
not be afraid. We choose our colors.

The other women bend to our feet,
and we go on talking produce, recipes,
the best way to pencil an eyebrow.

I look hard into every face coming through
security, she says, *because I don't ever want to see again*
what I saw then—people jumping to their deaths

to escape their deaths. Can you imagine
having to know a thing like that?

I remember the ivy,
the way it whiskered up the brick
of the hospital's old wing,
its broad red-edged leaves lifting
drowsily, like paws. So beautiful
and disturbing—its tenaciousness,
the way it seemed to insist climbing
was the only natural thing,
while across the lot
the new glass wing I waited in
shivered like a mirage, like a rib
that had been extracted from a cloud.
We don't need medics to push you,
these things run on tracks now,
the doctor said, and he looked familiar
in his white coat and corduroys,
explaining how now it was possible
to get a map of every illness you're likely to get,
or to die from, in your life.
I kept looking past him to the vines outside,
those burnt hands curling,
thinking it has always been frightening
to be alive, the way we can almost,
but never quite, remember the future.
I've traced fate on the underside
of a hand, and on a leaf,
but that was quaint, nothing
like it must have been once
to pass your palm across a table
to a reader you needed to believe.
It must have been something like this—
sweating under a paper gown,

swallowing blue fluid, buckling the body
and its unknown future to a table
that inches persistently forward
under slicing light.
Always this stillness
before you divine.

LOOKOUT

First we thought it was the shadow
of a duststorm or a swarm
of insects sliding over the ridge
and across the plains,
the way it darkened and rearranged
the land beneath. Then we saw
the massed particles coming closer
were not bug or buffalo
but people, carrying their young and old,
passing over the earth
as the earth was passing
in its own living skin.
And all this with a scorching
want that lowed in a loudening thunder.
Our tools were simple and carved from bone.
We held them fragile as artifacts, our eyes
smarted with dust and with sun
and we watched.

THE BONE

We found it in the garden,
beneath flint arrowheads and cooking tools,
scrapers of shining stone dent-shaped
by stone. The bone when tapped

rang out like glass and was so light
to hold, it may have been composed
of breath, space giving it shape
by way of endless inner catacombs,

brittle pocks we looked into
and saw as epochs of air
that had once been water,
once marrow, once bone.

One end had broken from its host
with the frayed desperate edge
of the death rattle or birth tear.
I could see where it had fought

not to be differentiated. The other
was a smooth knob I rubbed
like a talisman and felt long ago
rolling in a socket swaddled

in sinew, swiveling the hip
of some dark swift being.
I wrapped it in soft cloth,
carried it secretly to school,

checked it so often
it began to gleam
with my life, its shared air
a kind of hallowing.

CHEYENNE

I went down and down.
I swam beside the boat,
near its sucking wake and tall
dangerous sides. I pulled
through water hung with mud and slick
shale-stumbled banks running up to trees
and scattered logs bleached white by the sun.
The way I loved seemed to be confounding
everyone. I was not alone,
I had a friend I did not need language
with as we paddled side by side.
I was not shopping, scanning
the horizon for what would be a better life
but beside that ship of people
being ferried safe within their deaths.
We would all arrive at the same time,
but me by my own rhyming muscle.
I swam until the water grew warm
as a body around my body, until I was
in a liquid I had been before, I opened
my eyes against the current
and the stripping weeds, dragged myself
ever deeper into the strands of the past,
back to the riversplit where it all began
and scrambled out at last onto land
tingling with bramble and branch.
And you were there, and we were
strong-limbed and browning, and back.

MANZANITA

On the third day in the woods,
I empty—fill with cool mountain air
breathed from the pines.

You work to bank a fire.
You have cut yourself on a tree;
some thirst is slaked.

We have no tablecloth.
We split apples on the scarred wood.
Smoke flows into folds.

Our girl pretends to eat.
She lifts invisible morsels from the palm
of her hand, then sucks her fingers, *mmm.*

When I ask what she's eating,
she always says eggs.
There's a kind of power that's not power

over others. It comes from a weave
of the visible and not and appears
sometimes as a dignity, easy

to misunderstand.
I was once a daughter of the earth.
And once one who raped and colonized

the daughters of the earth.
It is not time that is the great teacher
but the way we understand time.

At least now I think our stories can begin
to turn back on themselves.

EURYDICE

Again, I have to tell our story.

I've been among the roots
and there's a warmth in the world
people have forgotten.

Inside the kettling bed and rotting
of everything that lives, it's hot
as my body.

Oh, I know how you looked for me
on streets, in the silhouettes of leaves,
how you lived on like a man

with your work and work
in the bonecold you call dread.
But we both had known you once

as me, and God,
were you heroic in your need,
coming back like that.

Then we set off
toward what you'd known
and it snapped—

what had I—
without you—
that fast flash

of cheek and what
did you see? Gleam
of my shoulder or knee?

Anyway.
They were live things
coursing with light.

It happened so fast:
me, made a part
in a gesture you'd call your own.

POMME

I had been trying to get out
all day. Death was boiling up in me
and I needed to walk into the golding
of redbud and burnishing ivy
climbing the walls like a long unknotting sigh.

He tore into the skin like a wolf.
And then no one, hardly anyone,
could step away from those
hot garnets pinned into flesh.

We ate the whole thing
standing up. I held my own
half like a cup and thumbed open
the pale dividing sponge,
and I plucked.

He sucked the seeds
through slick lips, tipped and drank
the pool of red.
Then the leathered sacks.
and brittling pulp. Stained lace,

a centerless form calling in low sun
and the ongoing landscape of want.

THE FLOATING DOCK

At the brim of the day and summer
and childhood, there is a floating dock.
Its sodden brindled planks tip drowsily,
rocking the kids who crawl then stand then slip
back to the molten bowl of silver,
an ocean scaled numb-blue and rose.
Its old glow fills the gullies
of the boys' backs and rounds
the girls' hips and flashing arms
as they slap and shove each other off.
Beauty's precipice is cruel.
One boy hangs from the side,
pulling seaweed slick as his sister's hair.
The tallest girl dives open-eyed,
spots fish and comes up calling.
More jump wildly, overeager,
laughing to follow as a flock
of seagulls chips and scatters out
like iron filings. A powerboat opens
its groan. Do they know?
This porous world will grow more so.

TWO

LATE SEPTEMBER

Gulls slide through the sky.

It's one of those days I've tried to get out
            into my actual life.

Late September and I don't even need art
            to heighten my seeing.

The low spotlight of the sun does it for me.
            Each blade of grass sidling up to its black.

Trees lapped by shadow and the Great
            Lake's frayed unending waterbreath

amid a yellowjacket hum
            and the whirring spin of crickets singing
we are all just river
            pouring over
the wheel.

From here, I can see them at the park.
            They are framed by the green ruffling
and all the times we will not be.

He leans against the slide reading a paperback.
            She climbs the red step.

He lifts her into the cup of the swing,
            and she throws her head back laughing.

I can't read their faces, only their forms.
            They have the same saturation into body
that turns the grass to stripes of light.

See, I am one of those who can't forget,
    who loves the one burning branch
turning the tree to something various and mortal,
    something true.

Who sees the world a long way off
    even when it's close
as this girl I love now running up.

KAUAI

We've come back to the site of her
conception. She calls it *why*

and cries all night,
sleepless, wild.

It seems the way is always
floating and the goal—

to live so the ghosts we were
don't trail us and echo.

I think we are inside a flower,
under a pollen of stars vast as scattered sand.

The air pulses with perfume,
flowers calling to flowers and the ferrying air.

But my eyes are thin and elsewhere.
I am thinking, maybe

even coming into the soul
is a difficult birth, squeezed by the body's vise.

My bent legs like pincers
or the vegetable petals of some tropical flower.

Even my mind gripped by the folds
of the flesh, how the cells keep twinning

themselves out toward complexity.
The tulip trees of the valley

spread their bone canopies into slick green leaves
and fire flowers deep as cups.

Their cups fill with rain, rain
drinks the leaves drinking rain.

I can't begin to explain.
How on this porous peak of stone in the sea

our daughter came into me.
Little flick of a fish I could not see.

I was just learning to be human
and upright among all that life.

And what was real was stranger
than night with its dust of unnamed suns.

It was the beyond in us.
And she was.

KALIHIWAI

I'm among the ochre-green
          and dying leaves, sitting amid the fecundity.
I tend to forget who I used to be,

fold on like water fizzing
          through rock that once was molten.
There's a sponge sound on the beach echoing

in my inner ear and black glands of stone
          and black glands like sand
on the backs of these veined, surrounding

leaves. Prehistoric, ferning, we are all
          afloat in a deep and foaming sea
of space tided by rolling fire.

And there is a way of listening
          to the even fall of water from a faucet
or body-breath of waves, the swell and recession

of a truck going by, or now
          the baby practicing her *o, ee, oo.*
She's clamoring up into language

and may always be, like me.
          A purple pod hangs like ballast
from the banana's knotted stalk,

its fruit soft and polyfronded
          as a mum cupped up.
So the bruised bell tolls the cord

of its purpose, a sweetening
        corpus of seed. Then a panic
in the windbreak and chickens

scattering dumb rust and iridescence.
        Of weight and wing, this offspringing
world is more than we

can imagine.

HELD

The yellow blanket swells and snaps against blue
sky and bluer white-throated waves.

The yellow is threaded with red
nerve-thorns and flowerings.

And there's a small girl laughing, peeking out
from under clapping cloth. She toddles off

on dented sand. It collapses
to the rippled tongue of sun

I toss my notebook on. She is one and who
knows what will stake the tent

of her memory?

I talked all afternoon to my friend.

After she pushed through the night,
breaking herself bloody to release
her child, the doctor botched-cut her up,
slicing anus to pelvic wall.

Now she can't lift her daughter.
Now pain climbs her to the teeth.
Now she lies with a digital wand
up her V and counts to ten
and tries to make a fist.

I wish love were more often
sourcing me. I wish there were a way
to get beyond all this.

Yesterday, I stood my daughter on the sill
and she pressed her hands
to the cold window.

People walking dogs.
Beige grass recovering
from the bludgeon of winter.

And just like that,
as if they'd summoned each other up,
a boy toddled down our walk
holding an orange.

They waved.
His a smooth sweep of color.
Hers a squeal and a knock on the glass.

Then his grandma smoking on the sidewalk
admonished him and called him back.

CREAM OF THE POUR IS THE CREAM OF SKIN THICKENING

I look out. Black leaves, color of dried blood
and my ulcerated tonsils flutter
as I breathe openmouthed. Through the branches
there are branches.

Some remember their lives
of green, some hang languorous
sturdy with sap.

The question becomes how to live
the right life, filling with it
like a liquid converted from light

until it becomes the weight
that factors your place
with gravity.

Until just walking to the car
you can sense suddenly, purpose

in traffic and glances, windswirls
coughing wrappers to the street

and that branch, quivering
as it touches another

which is also of course
itself.

MAYBE GRAVITY

is a metaphor for desire:
her attraction to the apple

and the star-seeded earth
inside it, the man

picking the fruit, dropping it
beside a hollow ball of twine

and watching the way bodies
of different weight

will even in air and land
at the same time,

as something in me is
falling now, knowing this

descent is cumulative
and has already been

parceled into an equation
elegant as the blossom

that mothers the fruit.
There will always be more to see,

I thought once, staring
into a grapefruit. *Everything missing*

will become something new.
Now I clop one open into two

sunny bowls, saw my knife
along the rim, tip it in and in

to the knot in the middle,
wedge a pink parcel onto my spoon

as juice and lashes of pulp
flood the gaps, splash me almost in the eye—

Yoo-hoo, why so far away? my mother
would call from the counter,

years before I understood
the measure of her attention,

her vigilance in dividing fruit from rind.
Now I shovel up mangled bits,

scrape the skin to a socket,
tear the pulp to raw rubbled mouth,

flaps and labia, lips of skin.
When isn't fruit a woman's body?

Years before the hot drop of menopause,
my mother held an apple in her elegant hand,

and in one uninterrupted turning,
stripped it of its sprung red ribbon.

We set it on the radiator to dry,
added a tiny kerchief and cloves for eyes,

and it was amazing, how soon,
how human its wrinkled face,

as if the doll were nothing we had made
but what had been there waiting.

OCEAN AND INTEGER

Shut out of sleep all week,
I unhinge from my body,
become a stirring in the stars
of my hands, those little quarrels
of bone and heat.

Thunder runs through the hall:
my daughter and her doll stroller
on the old wooden floors.

A little dripping in the kettle
and falling rocks of steam
in the pipes, and this may as well
be an essay on alchemy.

Yesterday, I took her to the pool,
submerged her little body
to hips, shoulders, chin,
astonished mouth.

Her training in freedom
must be incremental and guided
by my own radiant face
asserting its joys.

We swam then sang then seared
ourselves in the shower
and walked home through the farmers' market.

Corn bread in slick slabs,
amber jars of honey.

A woman with almond skin
and a shining crown of braids
bent to her bushel
and handed my girl a Red Delicious.

We ate that apple all day.
Its flesh was gritty as clouds
rolling low over water
and thick seeing.

It was just like poetry,
and when I say all day,
I mean we ate it right
down to the seeds.

After all that white body,
those pips of bitter wood on the tongue
can come as some relief.

LATE AUGUST

After you left for the airport we ran errands then got a rotisserie
chicken. I thought we'd have it with crusty bread and a salad of
baby greens, early apples and goat cheese. But the chicken was
tied with a string. It looked cold and too much like a body. I had
a memory it was going to pass us through its oil-soaked body.
I said I'm sorry, became a vegetarian again. It was the size you
were once curled in your mother then soon after huddled on her chest.
In that picture we have you're there in your face but your legs
look so thin they scare me. They scare me and make me want
to hold you and know what it was to put those tiny socks on you.
I think someday I will hold you and you will feel very frail to me.
I'm sure I will be afraid but I hope you will let me put aside
my fear for you. I hope I can. I hope a thing like that isn't
even in the room.

EUCHARIST

Today when you left I could not breathe.
My eyes folded up in me.

I had become the woman I thought
I would never be because

who would be worthy and besides
I'd never have the courage.

Now all the strength I trained for—
to not need—I need even more
to need you.

A child cries from our room.
She is not our daughter
but another coming

through the monitor
while ours sleeps beside me.

I break into a loaf of bread
as if it could be your body.

I think I understand it now.
I miss you in my mouth.

FIRED IN THE BODY

She cries and heat
pours my core into
the mouths she drinks from,
beading white.

Her hunger's a fear
of the new pain erupting
in her gums and inner ear

making her face an ancient
ruddy thing, its rhythmic
injured bleat repeating
my screams when I
broke to birth her.

That yell opened me into itself:
a churning current our body
rowed out and out on
until it hit the chopping sea
and was lost:

in her, seal-sculled and rooting,
and me, newborn beneath.

Now she jagged-paddles us up
over caps cutting the hull
as again and again she swallows

as if to take more of me
into her and inside-out
herself back into us.

In what she does not know
as words but tones, I say,
What's coming will be better.

It will be like fine earth
fired deep in the body,
the first bright chime of your power.

Soon you will not know
your mouth without it.

THE SECOND OF SEPTEMBER

I know this is not a poem.

I know this child trying out her vowels
is not our child.

They are like a woman
I saw in the mirror once.

I hardly remember her,
but I wrote her like a plume of smoke.

She must be close,
in some other house,
some other life, nearby.

What I mean is
this is not the poem our life is.

It breathes through the curtains.
The second of September.

I mean with you I am not lonely.

EQUINOX

At the dream's weeded fringe
the crone pauses, asks which of us now
is the one who cannot follow?

For years, I've walked the shaded circles
with her, led by the crooked branch of her finger.

Now I lay my infant daughter down
on a blue tarp over rotting leaves
and curled sleeves of birchbark
as she stares up through
the bruiseberry tree.

Purple buds that scabbed the branch
all spring are gone. New leaves
sigh green and shyly rearranging.

Pattered by their shadows, her face
flickers quickly my face—a faint layer
under her bolder gaze.

Somehow I have locked us out,
chasing after the older babysitter
with the watch she's forgotten
and the wrong key.

And suddenly, I am barefoot with a baby
and wool work clothes
in ninety degrees. At last,

I am not waiting or surviving, but alive
at the center of the woods
that ring us while we sleep.

ONE

And she's got a loneliness all her own,
a being like being

a lone wing dropped on asphalt quivering.

She sleeps in her own room, in a little crib
under blankets piled on like apologies.

She opens and closes her fist
in the grove of her own voice.

She does not know
the century. She does not think

she is the end of one thing
and the beginning of another.

She talks to the shapes light makes
as her mother moves in and out

of the rooms of being always partially
strange. She stares down the long corridor

of mothers, a hall of unmeeting eyes,
shuttered up, unrecognized.

The baby gurgles herself free.
The birthwater she swallowed

did not lodge in her heart.
She looks at me, through the bars,

as if to say, now
we have something more to do

than remember.

BIRTH IS WHEN WE RECALL OURSELVES

For a long time, all I could do
was think of those I was before.

Some of them wanted me back.

There was more we meant to ask,
they said. Remember.

Not all of us are born upside down.

I moved through the world
like someone in a strange hat.

Nonetheless a hoop of light shook loose in me
while I sat with my little needle,

air opening uncountable mouths to the thread.
Who said, some come with the mark

of the drift on their feet?
Like a slipstitch.

OFTEN SHE'D DROP INTO FATHOMLESS

Always I thought mother looking out the window
meant elsewhere meant longing

for self-wisps rippled in glass
and in the grass across the tracks beyond that.

I didn't know until you mother could be
me, looking out the window could be

this, third-person glancing it: joy
so whole she only hems it like a guest.

MILK

There's milk in me I do not see.
It ripens in little stills, it sleeps

in its body of bone, it waits for its host
mouth to call it out—into thread

tethering body to freshet, to river
moving through itself to river, to oceans

giving their skins up into rain.
I cannot taste it but sometimes

I lick her tears, my little ocean
spinning river into blood.

It is a heat in me, becoming me—
this giving.

IN THE SKIN TENT THE HEART WAS A FIRE

We saw yours across the fields,
its speech a scarf of smoke.

In the center of my life, I woke
flat on the bed, settling like a stone in my body.

My mother was in the next room,
drying her hairdo, wearing blue.

Soon she would draw the water
for my daughter's bath.

How had I grown so old
so young, surrounded by books,

mouthing poems over the face
in the long mirror, my bottom-half stippled

with my daughter's drumming
fingerprints, so my legs and feet

blurred into earth,
into a prairie stirred by the hooves?

White crack of apple on the board.
Smell of chrysanthemums, my mother's hands,

and an old knowing, wool-stiff
and wordless, braiding through us,

through the rooms.

THREE

THE SEA CAME UP AND DROWNED

It was the only way to live.

Usurp yourself to yourself
in waves, in centuries,

while something like truth
cooled below the surface in stone.

While something like a voice
began unwinding into the whorled pearl of its own home.

The earth is the earth and the memory
of water, every ridge a recollection

of water's recession.

*

In the middle of my life was fear,
a body of it, water

so cold it was stone and I rode it for years
not knowing I was moving

always around the void of the face
I had made. But it was life and not dreams

that pushed me finally through the spray.
I woke soaked and shaking,

having seen a truth partially caught in form
flawed and small, my arms

wet with what comes through
the skin, a liquor the nerves manufacture.

I tried to name it my god my child my love
murmured something meaning kindness

and I clung to him as ballast and went under
again into dreamlessness tiding dreams

I could not yet brave or catch, remember.

*

Those years stretched long and flat
as our palms, lined with grass,

wind-whipped, twisting tendrils of grass.
That was after we'd been grabbed

by history, after we'd entered our lives
through our dreams, our dreams

through the seams in our hands.
After they led us back here

to the prairie, the ocean's past
that splits us open like chaff,

where the grass chatters in the endless chatter
of the ancestors

and the unborn ancestors.

CONTAINER GARDEN

Talk stops in the self-conscious elevator.
The space is cramped and all the colors dim
referrals to oil, coal, steel—alloys
of growth and decay, drilled out
and burned against death into death.

Everyone's mute, gazing down
at their charcoal cuffs and tongueless shoes.
The prairie's gold robes, the sky's azure eye,
sunlight scratching the lake's wrinkled hide,
have all been dismissed as childish, too loud
for this palette of smog.

A drone and the doors slide open
to the rooftop of the future, which is now.
A hundred specimens of grass kept separate
in steel planters. Grass that once was grass
and now is any caged thing.

Once, a fish lent me her circular jaw
and I wore it as a crown, staring out
from a diadem of teeth. I lifted
it this morning from the tides of sleep,
brushed it off and cleared the weeds

to recall a current of beings who lived,
died, were eaten and ate with one mind.

Inward lush unpetaling purpose in pink blooms of sleep, and I no longer needed to be separate. I was living there then, at the edge of the sea. And my friends came to visit, trying for a baby, not sure how to read me on that island of dozy sunlight. And there it was: familiarity edged with fear, the way we'd feed each other sandwiches and wonder if we should have wanted something other. We walked the folded cliffs over conifer fronds and mud runneling rocks slick with dropped passionfruit and rotting camellias to pause at the first ridge. We looked through high pines at the blue moving tides, then his finger caught a snag in the water and another and we saw—glinting fins wheeling the sheen, thousands playing in pods coming closer like the souls slippering in to our bodies, attaching to matter as flippers angle in to a ferrying strand. We too are a species, I realized. We too could know that as joy.

AT THE DQ

Is the dream of the sod
just the dream to get out of the sod?

Did the geranium snapping its tonsils
against the Dairy Queen window
push upward in its pot for this—

to live, to look out
on a rust-covered crane
with its jaw full of rocks,
an awning burdened with wind,

two girls leaning against the picnic table,
licking swirly cones, aching
in the cores of their bones just to grow?

Is that why they're so quiet,
listening for gossip
to catch like sticky napkins in the wind?

They listen beneath a tree,
which sounds like far-off applause,
beside a river, which sounds like a woman

rushing to braid their shining hair,
pulling more and more length
from the stinging banks.

Soon it will swell over all it knows—
flat, clattering stones
etched with the delicate backbones

of creatures that lived,
then went extinct.

Whole hours when I forget about you.
I like the times we just admit it,

when I rock you in the creaking chair,
my arms heavy with us
each up in an elsewhere.

Your eyes like mine
stare not always seeing.

I was never afraid of solitude.
People made me flutter and unknow
myself but never the wild of being.

I had a love in college
I'd walk to at night, up steep wooded hills
through the graveyard and down again,
arriving at his place near morning.

Sometimes I'd see the eyes of creatures hovering.
Once a coyote just a few feet away.
I wasn't as afraid as I'd be of a man.

I'd stop to sleep awhile
under a tree and wake
in wet grass, that underskin blue
of just before dawn.

I loved the boy on the other side,
but I loved myself as much,
setting off like that, taking an apple
and some chocolate from my pack.

As a child sometimes, I'd look down
at my brown arm with its one mole
and faint down and my heart
would bolt forward in wonder.

I'd like to give you this.

The way darkness would seep
to the wicks of the trees, your life
gathers now in you.

I can see you already have it.

THE ENDANGERED SPECIES CAROUSEL

Lincoln Park Zoo, Chicago

Children wait in line, hopping,
hoping for their first choice—
a fiberglass panther waxed black as a car,
a panda smoking bamboo,
a harbor seal with velvety questioning eyes.
Measured by the bar, they clamber on,
beat their feet against the creatures' bellies,
say, *giddyup, hurryup,* while their parents smile,
wipe ice cream from their hands and mouths.
The recorded organ bells out clownish now, louder
as the animals shiver up and slide back down
on fat brass screws, threading the afternoon
with their tragic imagined grins.
Only the gorilla stays level,
looking down under lidded brows,
his heavy knuckles bolted to the floor,
and the boy on his manlike back looks worried
that he's only going round and round.
He's crying now. *It's okay,* his mother calls,
as he passes behind the lion, the swan,
the mandrill, the camel, *Don't worry, Hon,*
it's almost done!

LIKE PLAYING TWO INSTRUMENTS AT ONCE

Joy weeps over joy's
eventual end, hiding all the time
in the kitchen where I slice vegetables
and wash the rice.
My skin still smells like ours.
I can still listen as you open the piano,
drop each finger into a note, a world
we lived in once, like now,
in love. I went to you then
and my tears splashed onto the keys
and onto your wrists, salt stars
that burn long after they go out.
Now in evening, writing this,
I am that same woman—
the one who has lost you
and the one who will never lose you.
All day, the geese outside
shoved and bellowed over one on the ground.
It wasn't a keening but what I recognized
as life's complete disbelief.
They bit and bit at her white neck,
breaking it to make her rise.

Your body has begun its desolation
and probably will continue
to disintegrate, the therapist

said today, *in which case we will*
exercise ways to maintain your strength.
If the room is the present, ours betrays

hopelessness—ants teeming over a fallen
bit of apple, broken crayons and toys,
bags of recycling and trash.

Nothing grows here, nothing brightens
or expands. This kitchen is not my own,
this home is not my own.

What do we really own?
I hear you say, *not these spaces,*
these bodies borrowed in time.

If I enter your philosophy,
do I become a bone-flute
rattling on the sands again?

I did not want to come back
to that. You have odd logic, call it spirit,
make it serve tripe in stomach folds

to cold loneliness, it leaves me
tongueless, nothing, not a hollow bowl
stirred with sound, not white light stepping

from the hemfolds of form.
Let me recall our unknown
future with something like hope,

lying here with my blood trundling on,
trilling to my limbs' tips.
Let me imagine we will survive.

When you first welcomed me,
I thought, *mercy,* and wept
for what I did not yet know

how to receive, the sunrushed present
containing everything,
your wild heart tossing its beat at me—

I need, I need,
even the trees with their dark nerves
and thighs glittering ice,

steam singing from a kettle
lofting us footless as our daughter
still a speck beyond the surf.

All time and none, it was
breathing us in the breath
that's the breathe of the sea.

One by one your nerves will burn out
like bulbs in the muscles that
will no longer open your lungs.

And I'll be left in this
lone bone house raging
my best against ends.

CHILDREN TOGETHER

Okay, let's pretend our parents are dead,
one of us would say, and the games would begin.

In winter, we were squatting in a dim city
between furnaces and box springs, under spired pipes.

In summer, we were stranded on an island of tripweed and pine.
We chose our own names, agreed on our relations,

pulled dresses and vests from the trunk of old clothes,
listed the provisions we would scavenge and hunt,

then, as often as not, someone's mom would call out,
time to eat, time for so and so to go! and that would be it,

the whole game—planning to survive.

EARLY CHILDHOOD

was the morning infusing us
and borders more like fur
than surface, slurred
with sun and somehow spilling

into others, bowls into bowls,
as we sat in a half-moon circle
on the wooden floor.

That was in Indian-style,
with our legs over and under
in the trust that everything
was what we had to learn.

And so we listened
as the white-haired woman read
the words: *purple, juniper, bread* and *spoon.*

And she called each world good
in the way she held it—
its laminated spine
like the crackling stem
of a newborn's head.

Our heads then were huge
bone baskets made mostly of openings.
We leaned them into the moment
light crested and broke

into the forms of things,
shapes they taught us to memorize
while we felt their volumes filling up.

Oh, wasn't it the most gradual thing,
this sharpening into separate?

Remember when still my hand
in yours was either one?

HOUR

I rise from the table blinking,
still in the poem where every shape's

a music murmuring
on like water under rock.

You have entered the room,
but you are ages away from me,

fog-bellowed, mouthing.
I think I must have been born

to behold you like this,
from death's mist.

There are rings of humid light
around you—yellow-bearing-blue—

that have to do with where
the body ends. They hum

and humming how they hold you!

DOUBLE VISION

Sleep muddles me
>to memory

let me see
>it was a trick of muscle

a slackness snapping
>back the eye

into layered time
>a time-stammer

if time it is
>that bodies place

that world was
>the world before

specialists with
>their knives of light

cut me free
>I could see

through the page
>to the room beyond

and had to learn
>that things existed

this way—revealing
>what they were not

while remaining
         whole somehow

beside themselves
         and the days

shining through
         were real too

with real rooms
         holding real pages

and hands
         holding them

and all this
         would go on

opening to me
         in my body

if only I didn't try
         to grasp it dead-on

and dividing
         if only I'd let it

pool in me
         as an upcoming

clarity in a blurred
         circle I was

moving through
         it worked that is

when I could not see
         but only knew

THROUGH HOODED CLOUDS UNTRANSLATABLE, ONCE

I ploughed through sky toward it,
then after promise and partial

consummation, shadow purled
with knots of sun, I flew back again,

looking down on cobbles of white,
clods of mist in the heights.

I was flying! I had always been
myself and never more

than gathering and dispersal,
ever motion, ever flux, I have been

burdened by the very water
that will make me real.

And all this time, I've had only one
thing to do: learn to love.

My vaulted mouth splits
as that air enters me.

AFTER THE CAVERNS

On visiting a healer near Cave of the Mounds, Wisconsin

> *When I try to imagine a faultless love*
> *Or the life to come, what I hear is the murmur*
> *Of underground streams, what I see is a limestone landscape.*
> —W. H. Auden, "In Praise of Limestone"

The earth is a body.
Why were men so surprised
when their hungry plugs of fire
shot open the stone

to find water-carved caves,
bowls filled and sifted
with inner rivers ambered by
lime's radiant decay,

form maintained by its secret
of space? And is it too late to change
this world of hard, apparent shapes
by changing our perception of space?

You are energy, air, they say,
pure potentiality of atoms channeling
an unnamed vastness and all day
they charged you with this faith

while I traversed the murmuring
undersides of hills, walked sweating
ill-lit tunnels, slipped on hidden bridges
to emerge in the knifelight

of a precipice. I did not think
it would end. I did not say
your limbs will kiln to white to ash
to grass boning up some other life.

The fish, the bird,
their delicate spines,
are imprinted in us now as we drive
past fields furled with corn

and gold coils of hay,
in our steel pod, in our bodies
growing smaller now, scaffolded
by loss and the shocked explosions

loss makes known.
I pat your hand, you draw away,
and our day dissolves to movement
over land I have to steer sharp and fast,

with you unbuckled beside me,
asleep at last.

OZONE ALERT DAY

Heat like a caul I can't see out of,
        wading past the church with its burnished dome,
the florist and Polish deli, past a robin's bones

picked and drying in the road.
        I burned all morning reading, I burn
in my looking. *Love should stretch widely across all space*

and should be as equally distributed, Simone Weil wrote.
        A small girl tiptoes down the stoop, away
from her grandmother's cursing,

sings, *Adieu, adieu, es mucho mucho gusto,*
        to the Chinese worry balls sliding in her hands, trickling
their metal bells. Taught to speak

to no one, she multiplies
        among the daisies and black-eyed Susans,
milkweed pods nodding on the fence.

A woman shuffles by
        in a headwrap and long dress.
She presses a handkerchief to the darkness

of her neck, pulls her collar open to a wide raw wound,
        moaning softly, *oh.* I am close now,
I can see blood beading like burnt sugar

on her puckered skin. *Love*
        the one about whom you know nothing,
who could be lying naked, bleeding, unconscious in the road.

Clouds dissolve in the eye
            of this heat's needle. Tin flashes
in the woman's glance.

I should walk home quickly now,
            bring back water and a clean cloth.
Is it love, I wonder, only when it's pulled

live and aching through fear?

THE BRAIN OF THE WORLD WAS RECALLING
ITSELF

in a Polish deli on the northwest side of Chicago.
It had a kind of seeing and so perceived
the red, raw and broken all around.
Stubborn joint and gristle. The knife's bright
entitlement. And it wanted none—no
more—of this. It wanted only to open out
in combed formations.

All night the brain had sat regal as a cake in a case.
Then after the third shift, a man in a flannel
and workboots spotted with plaster walked up
and pointed at it—didn't even give it a name—

and an aproned woman slid her cold rubber-gloved hand
under and lifted it—quivering, gelatinous,
its viscid crenellations unfurling then
contracting—onto the scale.

It was heavier than it looked. It wouldn't be cheap.

She printed the label, set it on a small Styrofoam tray
and wrapped it in plastic, quickly, the way
they wrap the legs of the dead, to hold their shape,

while she thought of her husband at home—
he'd be up now, drinking coffee,
eating the sausages she'd left.
She hoped the way he'd begun to wheeze
when he came up the stairs
was nothing.

She didn't notice it fighting against the cellophane
with a sharp right jab and deep ongoing keening,
every chamber flexing, each
like a lung gulping freedom.

She just passed it to the man,
who grunted his thanks,
and if they'd ever noticed each other's faces,
now they forgot them.

The man carried it through the market,
through his weariness.
He grabbed an onion, fist-sized moon,
to bob in the broth around it,
knowing its translucent layers

would gradually part,
like a sweater from a blouse,
a blouse from a bra, the pearled husks
releasing a damp mass.

In an hour or two his wife would start the supper.
His kids would be up now, sitting mussed in pajamas
in front of a TV that goggled loudly
in the language he only understood in scraps,
the noise of it everywhere, dividing his life from theirs,
making his a kind of transparent, brittle peeling.

Under the plastic, it shivered, it pulsed;
it towed the man toward his long afternoon
and tossed a shy light, like plaster dust,
up onto his face, and anyone who saw him
carrying it, flashed fleetingly on flesh—

the chicken's cracked neck,
scrotum soft in the hand,
moonish sediment on the newborn's head,
her shoulder that first evening—

how it almost glowed, it was so pale,
a child would have guessed it was made of spun sugar,
an old woman would have said the purest fat,
the kind you can burn in a lamp if you have to
or spread on hard dark bread,

and anyone close enough to look
into the folds—would have felt strange,
as if they'd known all this already,
as if they recognized it from some throb behind the eyes.

I sleep alone as a pocket of air
swallows my skin, rolls me
between body and sheets.

I am far from you, floating,
a stone in a scream of space
while the sun our heart plods on

mostly unnoticed.
When it fails there'll be no way to keep
the heat, we'll freeze to nullity,

our skeletons runes scattered
in the shapes we once made.
Forms open to forms, rot's

an old growing we inherit
in the riddling. Rattle
in the radiator—death?—

or some presence we have not yet
imagined? I can't imagine
where you'll go when you've gone

over the folds, the old
stories say, to the people
of the stars, the sun—

LA PORTE

In the seam between day and night, wind
          ruts the dirt road and
ruffles the milky way of dandelions.

The young among them are greasy gold and urgent,
          while the old are balanced
between growth and that explosion past

growing—annihilation, culmination
          of a beginning each has always been
ending toward, admitting more and more

space, until what's left is
          beyond color, a bleary truss
of matter and air. Shocked

accomplice of the rounding light,
          how you tremble in the stretch
of your death, which is like all deaths,

geometric with seed. Wind-swimmer,
          eye-floater, white-nightgowned grandmother
dancing your platelets on the head of this pin,

can you show me how to wish,
          how to gather and scatter
this single hooped breath?

IT HAD TO END

We aren't given heaven
just to keep it.

We get the sand
passing through our fingers

and even as it goes, the mind
trying to keep up, to remember

its quick glintings and
purr of an inner ocean.

A child digging basins
in the beach thinks,

We are all just sand
shaken in a hand

everyone whispering,
Listen. Her mother

looking up into sun—
We loved

full and momentarily,
a cupped flame fed

by what we could not be.